Short Promo Success

How to Run Successful Free Book Promotions in
Just One Day

by Dan DeFigio
IronRingPublishing.com

Table of Contents

Introduction

Despite Kindle's huge success, the self-publishing market is still growing. That's good news, because it means there is a BIG market for writers and publishers. Amazon is the largest book retailer in the world.

As a self-publisher, be it part-time or full-time, the Kindle movement provides you with a great chance to unleash your work to the world – and hopefully to make some extra cash too! With more and more Kindle-friendly devices being sold every year, the amount of people reading Kindle products is also increasing.

However, the ease and popularity of self-publishing also means that there are a lot more books for readers to choose from. More every day. A LOT more. How are you going to get your book to stand out amongst the millions of other titles available?

A big part of being successful on the Kindle platform involves knowing how to promote your work. Thankfully, Amazon has devised a great tool to help self-publishers get their books seen by readers – Amazon Kindle Direct Publishing promotional days! Promo days can help your new book get noticed, get off the ground, and gain traction.

What The Short Promo Success System Has Done For Me

The system I am about to share with you reliably pushes a new, self-published book into the top #1000 Free (and often into the top #300 or #400 Free) using a single Amazon Free Promotion day. It also typically gets the books onto multiple bestseller lists.

Just so you know, I am not one of these writers who promise that his miraculous system will skyrocket your Amazon listing into thousands of sales with no effort on your part! This how-to book is just about running an effective one-day Amazon free promotion to start getting some traction for your new book.

This system is just one of many effective systems of promoting your self-published book. A single successful Amazon promotion does not guarantee future sales or rankings. Books need consistent marketing and promotion in order to sell consistently! This system will simply teach you a reliable way to start getting some traction on Amazon's KDP platform for your new book launches with a simple and inexpensive initial promotion day. Read on to learn how!

About Kindle Select Free Promotions

In writing this how-to booklet, I am assuming that you, the reader, are either relatively new to self-publishing, or you have been unsuccessful in your promotional endeavors so far and need some guidance as to how to get your KDP promotions to perform better. The following section is a quick summary of how Amazon's free promotions work. Readers who are very familiar with Amazon's KDP platform can skip this section and go right to the *How Amazon's Ranking Algorithms Work* section – you don't want to miss that one!

What are Amazon KDP Promotional Days?

Kindle Direct Publishing (KPD) days are days when you give your book away for free. This allows new books to enjoy more visibility by encouraging people to read a new book at no charge.

This system is optional, which means enrollment in it is completely voluntary.

The Advantages of Running Promos

There are several advantages to taking part in the Amazon KDP promotional system. The first is exposure. There are millions of titles listed on Amazon, and it's very hard to get your book to stand out. Getting on any of Amazon's lists that they display to customers (in this case, a list of books about a certain topic that are free) really helps narrow the playing field.

This exposure also helps customers find other books you've written or published. If you currently have multiple kindle books for sale on the Amazon marketplace, your overall sales will likely benefit from having more people check out your other work.

Because you're offering one of your books for free, many more people will download it, read it, review it, and check out your other titles. As your book becomes popular in your categories, you'll rank on Amazon's Best Seller charts (assuming you reach a certain amount of sales). This only increases the amount of exposure you'll get, which will hopefully turn into sales!

Getting your book on Amazon's Paid Best Seller list is the veritable gold mine that all authors and publishers seek.

While you don't make any money while your book is being given away for free, your book's activity on Amazon – the browsing and downloads your book has received – is charted in Amazon's system and affects your book's perceived popularity, making it more likely that the Amazon algorithms will display your title more often.

The Downside to Promos

In order to be able to use Amazon's KDP promotional tools – Free Promotional Days and Countdown Deals (I don't discuss Countdown Deals in this book), you'll need to enroll your title in Amazon's **KDP Select** for a 90-day period. This gives you access to the promo tools, and it also automatically enrolls your book in the Kindle Owner's Lending Library so that people can lend and borrow it at no charge (and you'll get paid if they read it).

The downside to enrolling your book in KDP Select is that you are giving Amazon the exclusive right to sell your work in digital format. During this 90-day period, you cannot sell your book on any other electronic platforms, such as iBooks, Nook, or Kobo. You can still distribute printed copies via any other channel, though.

Choosing Your Free Promotion Days

One of the good features of KDP free promo days is that you're allowed to choose your promo days. Opt for
Christmas Day if you'd like, or New Year's Day, or any of the other 363 calendar days. The choice is yours. You're allowed 5 free promotional days in each 90-day KDP Select enrollment period, and you get to decide when you want your book to be given out for free, and for how long. You can use up your promo days consecutively if you choose to, or use up your days one at a time over the course of the 90 days. It is my mission in this book to teach you **how to run a successful promotion using just one of your free promo days!**

Promo days don't roll over. After 90 days, the 5-day allotment resets, and any promotional days you didn't use are lost. Amazon only gives you 5 promotional days per enrollment period, so be sure to use all your precious promo days within the designated time frame!

Long vs Short Promotions

Many successful authors and publishers run Amazon free promotions for several days in a row. These types of promotions can certainly be successful and build a lot of momentum for your book, but the purpose of this instruction is to teach you how to run a very successful promotion in just one day. I encourage you to explore the longer promotion strategies after you have had some successes with the simple Short Promo Success system.

How Amazon's Ranking Algorithms Work

Although Amazon's ranking algorithms are closely guarded trade secrets, here's what we've been able to reliably figure out:

- External ads only need to drive above-average sales volume over a short timeframe in order to improve rank.

- The algorithms reward upward trends, and seem to drop anything that isn't trending upwards. So if your 3-day promo peaks on day 1 or day 2, your momentum can disappear overnight and the whole effect can be lost. This is why I generally use one-day promos and decided to share my system with you!

- The faster the climb, the more Amazon's algorithms will boost your results. Big spikes of activity seem to catch Amazon's eye more than slow-and-steady improvements – another good reason to start with powerful one-day promotions.

- The higher the pre-promo starting rank, the greater the subsequent rank boost and the longer that boost lasts.

- Higher numbers of Amazon customer reviews appear to boost the positive effects of the above, but exactly how much is not yet clear. There is much debate about this on the self-publishing discussion forums. At the time of this writing, it appears that books with 30 or more reviews get a boost in the Amazon book rankings.

- Borrows on Kindle Unlimited influence the sales rank immediately – you don't have to wait for the reader to get through 10% of the book for your rank to increase.

Step-By-Step Checklist For Short Promotion Success

1. Publish your book with an eye-catching, easy-to-read cover. Don't skimp on your cover design – it is
2. the single most important thing that will affect your sales (until you're famous enough that your name trumps an unappealing cover)!

3. Your book description is the second vital component of successful sales and promotions. Your Amazon description must outline benefits to the reader, and you must write a compelling reason for them to pick up your book instead of the literally millions of other options. Consider using Derek Doepker's service to help write an irresistible description (Derek is the creator of the Hooks For Books system, and he can be reached at info@ebookbestsellersecrets.com.

4. Price your new book at $.99 for now.

5. Purchase 5 gift copies and email to people you can (hopefully) count on to write a favorable review. It's very helpful to have at least a handful of positive reviews before you start your first promo. If you have some publishing colleagues, you can do some 99-cent review swaps with each other.

6. Schedule your one-day promo via the KDP Dashboard at least 8-10 days away. (If you don't know how to do this, visit kdp.amazon.com/help?topicId=A34IQ0W14ZKXM9)

   My best results have been running one-day promos on Wednesdays or Thursdays.

7. Fill out this Data Sheet for your book:

   Author name: Link to free book:
   Author email: Free start date:
   Book Title: End date:
   Book Description: Your Amazon author page:
   Category suggestions: Tweet for your free book:
   Author Bio: A unique book description for
   Amazon ASIN: JustKindleBooks.com:

11

8. At least one week in advance of the promo date, I have my assistant schedule free promotional listings on these 50 sites, using the information from the above Data Sheet:

armadilloebooks.com/submit-free-ebooks/

awesomegang.com/submit-your-book/

blackcaviar-bookclub.com/free-book-promotion.html#.UXFB27XYeOc

bookangel.co.uk/submit-your-book/

bookcanyon.com/submitbook/

bookdealhunter.com/submit-free-book/

bookgoodies.com/submit-your-free-kindle-days

bookpinning.com/?sws=home/submit-book

bookpraiser.com/submitbook/

bookzio.com/tall-book-promotion/

contentmo.com/submit-your-free-ebook-promo

dealseekingmom.com/about/contact/

ebookasaurus.com/free-book-listing/

ebooklister.net/submit.php

ereadergirl.com/submit-your-ebook

ereaderiq.com/contact/

ereaderlove.com/contact/

free-stuff-unlimited.com/contact-us-2/

freebookdude.com/2014/03/list-your-free-amazon-kindle-books.html

freebooks.com/submit/

freebookshub.co.uk/authors/

freebooksy.com/editorial-submissions

freeebooksforme.com/authors-page/

freehomeschooldeals.com/submit/

frugal-freebies.com/p/submit-freebie.html

igniteyourbook.com/free-ebook-submission/

iloveebooks.com/for-authors.html

indieauthornews.com/p/contact-us.html

indiebookoftheday.com/authors/free-on-kindle-listing/

itswritenow.com/submit-your-book/

jungledealsandsteals.com/submit-your-kindle-freebie

jungledealsandsteals.com/submit-your-kindle-freebie/

justkindlebooks.com/submit-your-book (Use the UNIQUE DESCRIPTION for this site)

kindlebookpromos.luckycinda.com/?page_id=283

lovelybookpromotions.com/?page_id=124

onehundredfreebooks.com/author-free-kindle-book-submission.html

pretty-hot.com/submit-your-book/

sweetiespicks.com/free-kindle-books/

authors.ereadernewstoday.com/

bookbub.com/submit-order/new

docs.google.com/forms/d/1TrchfuOqR-xYMqfNBmlmi2TD9uLWavhzLyAwV8sWLTw/viewform

docs.google.com/spreadsheet/embeddedform?formkey=dGktOG5xb EZDYVVBUFE1S21DZUxoeFE6MQ

Send the Tweet to these twitter accounts:

01. @freebookclub1
02. @ibdbookoftheday
03. @Booksontheknob
04. @bookbub
05. @kindle_free
06. @freeebooksdaily
07. @kindlefreebooks
08. @zilchebooks
09. @freedailybooks
10. @free2kindle
11. @freereadfeed
12. @digitalinktoday
13. @fkbt
14. @kindlestuff
15. @Bookyrnextread
16. @CheapKindleDly
17. @free_kindle_fic
18. @DigitalBkToday
19. @kindlenews
20. @ebook
21. @freebookdude
22. @pixelofink
23. @IndAuthorSucess
24. @IndieKindle
25. @kindleebooks
26. @Kindle_promo
27. @freeebookdeal
28. @free

29. @free_kindle
30. @4FreeKindleBook
31. @FreeKindleStuff
32. @KindleBookKing
33. @KindleFreeBook
34. @KindleUpdates
35. @KindleDaily
36. @WLCPromotions
37. @free_uk_ebooks

Remember, using many sites to drive traffic to Amazon will boost your rankings more than using just a few sources!

9. The night before your scheduled free promotion, double-check that your book is scheduled to be free via your KDP dashboard!

10.   The day before your scheduled free promotion, price your book higher than you planned for your "normal" price. For example, if you intend to

normally price your book at $2.99, raise the price to $4.99. The reason for this is to give a greater perceived value of the free download.

11.   Do a little hashtag research on twitter and Facebook. You'll need a handful of popular tags that are relevant to the subject matter of your book for your Day-Of posts tomorrow!

What To Do On The Day Of The Promotion

1. First thing, check to make sure your book is indeed FREE on its Amazon page! Every once in a while, there are software bugs in the Amazon system, and you'll end up with a scheduled promotion not starting. If this happens, email KDP customer support immediately and ask them to put the book on free promo for you. You'll get a late start, but it will be OK.

2. Early in the day (around 7:00 am or 8:00 am Eastern Time), post your free promotion to the following sites:

   reddit.com/r/FreeEBOOKS/

   freebooksifter.tumblr.com/submit

   kboards.com/index.php/board,42.0.html

   freebookclub.org/kindle-books/book-submissions

   addictedtoebooks.com/content/todays-free-kindle-books

   booksonline.directory/freeaddyourbook.php

   kornerkonnection.com

   bookpinning.com/?sws=home/submit-book

3. Post your free promotion on the following Facebook pages (you'll need to join most of these groups in advance):

   facebook.com/freekindlebookz
   facebook.com/ourawesomegang
   facebook.com/BookGoodies
   facebook.com/TheWritePromoStuff
   facebook.com/ReadersRetreat
   facebook.com/TheWritingNetwork
   facebook.com/groups/748856645171748 (non-fiction only)

facebook.com/groups/FreeEbookGroup

facebook.com/groups/bookjunkiepromotions

facebook.com/groups/booksgoneviral
facebook.com/groups/294455560643884

facebook.com/groups/ebooksrock

facebook.com/groups/270558336379692
facebook.com/groups/320356974732142

facebook.com/groups/1577441379149696

facebook.com/groups/boomdom

facebook.com/groups/freekindlebookclub

facebook.com/groups/freetoday

facebook.com/groups/Kindlepromo

facebook.com/groups/bookplace

facebook.com/groups/512098985483106

facebook.com/groups/179494068820033

facebook.com/groups/2204546223

facebook.com/groups/borntowrite

facebook.com/groups/KindleFriends

facebook.com/groups/481534748544531

facebook.com/groups/BooksLuvers

facebook.com/groups/passionforbooks

facebook.com/groups/fabfridaypromo

facebook.com/groups/370900356880

facebook.com/groups/apablog

facebook.com/groups/BookPromotion

facebook.com/groups/443014452450161

facebook.com/groups/freebkrus

facebook.com/groups/135486133130440

Here are some important tips for Facebook posts:

- Write an engaging summary/teaser of the book. Readers have <u>thousands</u> of free books to choose from every day. MAKE someone want to download your book, don't just throw your link out in a post!

- Include relevant hashtags for the subject matter of your book in your post, along with an assortment of these suggested tags:

  #freeebook

  #freebook

  #freekindle

  #kindleunlimited

  #amazonkindle

- Include the US link to your free book on Amazon.com near the top of your description (so it can be clicked before the "See More" cutoff), and add an invitation to share, such as "feel free to share this link if you like."

- Put the US ink at the end of your post too, along with a simple call to action like "Get it now while it's FREE!"

- Include the links to your book's UK, Canada, Australia, and India Amazon pages at the end of your post. If your book would be particularly appropriate for a reader in a different country, include that country's Amazon link too, if it exists.

- Don't be selfish. Download other free books from these sites. Make comments. Write reviews. Share interesting books on your social network pages. Engage with the community, and help each other out!

4. Tweet your free promo to the following:

  @DigitalBkToday

  @kindleebooks

  @Kindlestuff

  @KindleUK

  @KindleBookKing

@KindleFreeBook

@KindleFreeBooks

@kindlefreebookz

@FreeReadFeed

@4FreeEBooks

@FreeBookDude

@4FreeKindleBook

5. At around 3:00 pm Eastern Time, re-price your book back down to $.99. This will encourage maximum sales after you end your promo. People who missed getting your book when it was free may still buy it at 99 cents. They may not if it's back to full price. You want as many purchases as possible right after your free promotion ends!

6. Later in the day (I do it around 4:00 or 5:00 pm Eastern Time), you can re-visit each of the Facebook pages, search for your book, and bump your post by writing a comment. Alternatively, you can delete your morning's post and post a fresh one. Don't have more than one active post per day on each page!

7. Check your book's ranking around 5:00 pm Eastern Time. You should be better than #1000 free by now (or at worst, very near the #1000 mark). End your promotion immediately if it's in the top #100 Free. If you're between #1000 and #100, watch your ranking carefully every hour (refresh your browser page!), especially if you've broken the top #500. Remember, what we want is to end the promo on an upward trend.

   End your promotion when:

   Your book rank worsens, even a tiny bit (i.e. free ranking drops from #225 free to #253 free)

   OR

   It's 9-ish pm Eastern Time and the rate of your rank improvement has been minimal for the last two hours (for example, at 7 pm your book was #324, and at 9:00 pm it's at #311)

Running a successful promo isn't a miracle-maker for your books, but this fast, inexpensive system will reliably break your free books into the top few hundred (assuming that it's a popular topic), and likely lead to some nice sales for at least the next few days!

Lend This Book For Free –
and Please Review

Amazon Prime members can lend and borrow books for FREE! (you also get free two-day shipping, and **unlimited** movie and TV streaming!)

And while you're on Amazon,
please leave a review – let other readers know what you liked about this book!

Reviews are very important to authors like me.

Thank you!

Free Tips for Publishers and Authors

As a special thank you for reading this far, I'd like to share with you a pile of free advice, t ps, and techniques for publishing success. I have a large network of colleagues who have been very successful in self-publishing, and they've given me permission to share some of their very best stuff here. Sign up to get schooled! Visit IronRingPublishing.com/publishers

Other Recommended Books

Visit **IronRingPublishing.com** to sign up for notifications of new releases, free books, and other special giveaways!

5 Minute Marketing For Authors

by Barb Asselin

If you have books to promote and **no time**, this book can help. Inside you will find:

- An explanation of book promotion strategies that can take only 5 minutes a day to perform
- A list of "to do" items that are recommended to be completed before you start the 5-minute marketing plan
- A 90-day marketing plan for your book that only takes 5 minutes a day to complete, and
- A customizable Word template so that you can create your own 90-day, 5-minute marketing plan!

Hooks For Books

By Derek Doepker

The most important keys to making your kindle books bestsellers, written by a guy who does it EVERY TIME!
Read about Derek's Must-Have system here:

jvz3.com/c/375641/90537

Disclaimer and Terms of Use

The author and the publisher do not hold any responsibility for errors, omissions, or interpretation of the subject matter herein, and specifically disclaim any responsibility for the effectiveness or appropriateness of any methods or advice presented in this book. This book is presented for informational purposes only. Always consult a qualified professional before undertaking any publishing endeavors.